ALL YOU WANTED TO KNOW ABOUT

How to Prepare Your Will

R. N. LAKHOTIA
SUBHASH LAKHOTIA

New Dawn

NEW DAWN
a division of Sterling Publishers (P) Ltd.
A-59, Okhla Industrial Area, Phase-II, New Delhi-110020
Tel: 6916165, 6916209, 6912677, 6910050
Fax: 91-11-6331241 E-mail: ghai@nde.vsnl.net.in
www.sterlingpublishers.com

All you wanted to know about How to Prepare Your Will

ISBN 81 207 2398 8

Reprint 2004

Published by Sterling Publishers Pvt. Ltd., New Delhi-110020.
Lasertypeset by Vikas Compographics, New Delhi-110020.
Printed at : Sai Early Learners (P) Ltd.

Contents

The Authors

R.N. Lakhotia is a well-known authority on taxation in the country. He is a regular writer and editor of several books on income tax, vegetarianism, better living and humour. His various books have seen over 400 editions so far. He is the founder President of Income tax Payers Association, Rajasthani Academy and Life Trustee of Hindi Bhawan, and is active in social and cultural activities. He is the former-District Governor of Lions International. He is the Principal of

Lakhotia College of Taxation and Management. As the Life Patron and President of Indian Vegetarian Congress, Northern India, and Editor of "Excellent Living", a monthly journal, he is spreading vegetarianism for health and happiness. He writes a regular column "Tax Doctor" for *The Times of India*, every Tuesday, and answers tax questions every Tuesday at Zee News (Business) channel.

Mr. Subhash Lakhotia is an income tax practitioner for over 30 years. He writes regularly for various national dailies, including *The Economic Times*. He is the Director of Lakhotia College of Taxation and Management and Editor of "Tax Saver", a well-known monthly journal on tax planning and tax saving. He is a practising consultant on tax planning, tax documentation and investment planning. He conducts the popular course known as "Zero to Hero in Income tax". He was regularly seen for 18 months on 'Business News' on Zee TV and on other channels conducting programmes on Personal Tax. He also writes a regular "Tax Talk" column for *Hindustan Times*.

What is a Will?

One of the most important requirements of a person having valuables/assets, is to write a will. Yet this is a necessity that is often neglected.

After a person's death, his assets are disposed off either as per the intentions of the deceased, or in the event that his intentions are not known, through the legal process of inheritance.

A person can make his intentions known by executing a Will. A person making a will may safeguard his interest during his lifetime by not making the will public. He can treat it as a 'secret document', to be read only after his death.

If a person dies intestate, that is without making or writing a will, then his assets, both movable and immovable, will be divided amongst his legal heirs, as per the provisions contained in the Hindu Succession Act. Those who do not fall under the Hindu Succession Act are governed by their personal law or the Indian Succession Act. In such a case, the properties/assets may not be distributed logically or in a most advantageous manner, but by strict application of law.

However, it is not possible to keep in abeyance the inheritance nor can there be disinheritance of the assets of the dead person. But when the person prepares a will, then he enjoys the opportunity of distributing his assets in the manner he considers appropriate and just. Thus a person preparing a will is in a position to divide all his movable as well as immovable assets amongst different family members and other relatives in the ratio of his choice and suitability of recipient.

A will is not an irrevocable document. It can be changed by the executor, whenever he so desires. No matter how many times he makes a will in respect of a particular asset, it is his last will or the one that has the latest date, that will be valid.

A legal owner may give away his assets exclusively to one member of the family or divide his assets between different family members in different ratios. Whether the distribution of the assets through a will is reasonable or not, it cannot be challenged by anyone. Even the legal heirs or the person receiving the assets through a will cannot challenge the will if they find that they are in receipt of assets much lower than what they would have inherited, had there been no will. Their plea will not be taken into consideration. However, the person preparing a will must be of sound mind at the time of writing his will and it should be a genuine one. As the disposition of the assets is to take effect only after the death of the person, he need not tell anyone anything about his will.

If a will is prepared by a person but not actually executed, (signed by him and the two witnesses), then in the eyes of law, it will be treated as if there is no will, and assets will be distributed amongst the legal heir(s) as per the prevailing law and the law applicable.

The author of a will or the person preparing a will is known as a testator. A testator must draw up his will with full freedom, devoid of any pressure and coercion from any person or relative. However, preparation and execution of a will must be done with a sound mind. A will executed with unsound mind is not valid. A person with unsound or weak state of mind cannot make a proper will. Therefore, it is better that in the preamble to the will, it is clearly written that the person preparing the will is of sound mind and that the will is prepared without any persuasion or coercion.

The person preparing a will is also at full liberty to revoke his will at any time. If he likes, he can make another will. However, if he does not make a new will and only cancels or revokes the earlier will, then the succession of assets amongst the legal heirs will take place as per the Hindu Law or the general law of succession.

A will is a very secret and confidential document, with the basic aim of providing a legal platform for distribution of his assets to various members of the family after his demise. A will may be made on a stamp paper or a plain paper. It is not necessary to register a will. However, it is always better that the will is registered at the office of the sub-registrar. A will may also be notarized. A person preparing the will must sit down calmly and list his broad assets. Then he should calculate, who needs what, or which of his assets are beneficial to who, or whom he would like to give the specific assets. Based on this, the distribution of the assets can be demarcated through the process of the will. For example, a person has a family comprising of himself, his wife, two major sons and two major daughters. All the children are well settled and married. Suppose he desires to give away Rs. 15 lakhs to his wife, and the balance amount to his sons and daughters, he can do so by writing his intention in the will. However, if he does not make a will and were to die intestate, then his assets would be divided amongst his wife and four children in equal proportion. Which of the two options is more desirable? The testator's intentions will make a difference.

When a will is prepared, the testator has full control on the distribution of his assets and he should put his desire on paper for the desired results.

It is recommended, that the present assets of the person preparing a will are duly recorded in the will itself with a clear-cut direction of inheritance of these assets by different members of the family. At least two persons must sign a will as witnesses. This is an essential requisite for a will to become a valid document. Any adult person can be a witness. It is possible in a family to save income tax by planning a will. In the subsequent chapters, we shall go through a journey of tax planning through the process of creation of a will. For example, a person who is preparing the will has a son and a wife. If there was no will, both the son as well as the wife would have inherited the assets in equal proportion. But if the will is prepared with proper planning, may be, it would be better to distribute the assets not to the son but to the wife of the son, as well as to the children of the son. Just with this kind of planning, he can ensure that too much money is not lost on takes.

New income tax files can be created through the process of a will, specially the file of discretionary trust. A new Hindu Undivided Family (HUF) can be created through a will in case there is a specific intention of the executor to transfer a portion of the assets to the HUF of a family member. Similarly, the income tax file of a person who is dead can legally be continued at a later point of time in the event of the preparation of the will.

Through a will, a trust can also be created while the funds can also go to some existing trust. Similarly, the funds can also go to the HUF. When the assets are proposed to be distributed to persons other than individuals, like certain trusts and HUFs, it is better if in the will a clear-cut mention of these trusts and HUFs is spelt out. If the trust or HUF is not existing as on the date of the will, but the same is created for the first time by the person preparing the will, then it is better that the will itself contains full details with regard to the objects of the trust, the beneficiaries of the trust, the ratio of income distribution in the trust, the powers and the duties of the trustees, etc. Similarly, if certain funds are proposed to be given away to the HUF which may not be existing as on that day, then the will should clearly speak about the names of various beneficiaries and the members of the said HUF, the rights and duties of the members of the HUF and the conditions regarding investments or otherwise, by the HUF, in respect of the funds so inherited.

If certain funds are proposed to be spent on charities, a will should clearly speak about the charitable trust or organisation to whom the funds are to be given for charity. If the person preparing a will has got in mind some specific area of charity, the same should specifically be mentioned in the will. For example, a person is interested in giving one lakh rupees for charitable purposes, but he is specifically interested in helping handicapped persons, then he must clearly write down that the amount is to be given away only for helping the handicapped. The choice of mentioning the charity trust or the funds to whom the funds have to be given away lies with the person preparing the will. He may specifically mention the name of the charity trust to whom the money has to be given by way of charity.

In tune with the changing times and also in tune with the

uncertainties prevailing in the world, you find life is not certain. It is better, therefore, that every person, generally after the age of 45 or 50 years, prepares a will and registers it. By doing this, a person does a great service to his family and loved ones so that the future generation does not fight among themselves on the mode of succession or inheritance. By preparing a will the person does not lose anything, rather he gets a rare opportunity to use and apply his own mind and distribute his assets, even though the implementation work will take place only when he is not alive. Thus, the person preparing a will continues to enjoy full control of all the assets in his possession which are mentioned in the will with not a single rupee being distributed amongst any of the family members. There is no single reason for non-preparation of a will. Besides, as mentioned above, preparation of a will and changing a will depends on the needs of the family, the testator's state of mind, mood and relationship with other family members. Through the process of the will the testator will leave no uncertainties about succession and inheritance.

A will may contain meticulous details about distribution of assets among beneficiaries. A testator can also narrate his/her personal feelings, love and affection about other family members through a will which could become a historical document for the family in years to come. When we are dead and gone, no one will be able to know what feelings we had in our mind about the other members of our family, but through the will it is possible to capture the feelings in written document, in black and white.

It is not necessary to mention in a will, why a particular person has been deprived of a share in the property of the person preparing a will. Similarly, it is not necessary to mention the reason why a particular person has been given a higher share of his assets. If, however, the person preparing a will wishes to write the reasons for his dividing the property in a particular manner, he may do so.

A will can be written in Hindi or in English or in any other language. If a will is written on a plain paper, virtually no expenditure is incurred to register a will. The expenses for registration at the Registrar's office are very nominal.

With the changing trends in society and to avoid all hassles, tensions and fights amongst the family members regarding your assets at a future point of time, the best solution and answer is a Will.

Advantages of Making a Will

There are innumerable advantages of making a will. It is a very well-known fact that if a person dies without making a will, his or her assets will devolve on the legal heirs and take the legal course as contained in the Indian Succession Act or other acts and rules by which a person is governed. Reversely, when a person prepares a will, then it supersedes all the provisions of law relating to inheritance of the assets. Thus the biggest advantage in favour of preparation of a will lies in the mobility in distribution of the movable and immovable assets. As a result of this, a testator has all the power and authority of doing whatever he wants with his property. In other words, full discretion lies with the person preparing the will to distribute his assets as per his intentions, even if a will is changed again and again.

Another big advantage of the preparation of a will is the encashment of the freedom available to a person to dispose of his assets in tune with his own thinking and perception. Imagine, a person who possesses a lot of wealth but does not prepare a will and dies intestate. His assets are distributed among the legal heirs as per the provisions of the law concerning succession. This person did not enjoy the freedom which was available to him to distribute the assets by application of the mind. He did not judiciously apply his mind in distribution and use of assets which he had accumulated through his hard work.

A testator can express his appreciation for relatives and legal heirs in his will. Through a will it is also possible to reward a person, whether a relative or a non-relative for his sincerity, loyalty and affection. For example, a person who was very attached to his servant who looked after him in his old age rewarded the servant with monetary gains and also appreciated all that the servant did for him through his will. In the absence of the will, this faithful servant would have been left unrewarded and those who did not care for the old man would have got everything. Thus, through a will, it is easy to award or reward and provide monetary benefits to relatives, friends and well-wishers by allocating a portion of assets for them on his demise.

Another advantage of preparing a will is the ability to bridge the gap between the rich and the poor legal heirs. Sometimes some of the legal heirs are very rich while others are not so rich. In the absence of a will, all family members would inherit proportionately the assets through the process of the Hindu Succession Act. But with a will, it is possible to bridge this gap and allocate funds and assets depending on the need. For example, if Mr 'A' has two sons 'X' and 'Y'. The wealth of Mr 'A' is Rs. 40 lakhs. Now 'A' finds that one of his sons Mr 'X' possesses income and wealth running into crores of rupees, while his other son 'Y' is just able to make both ends meet and that also with great difficulty. While 'X' has got two grown up sons, 'Y' has one daughter of marriageable age. In this situation, if Mr 'A' wanted to provide more funds for the family of 'Y', it would be possible only if the will is prepared. It is through the will alone that Mr 'A' may allocate a major portion of the funds to the family of 'Y', keeping in view his present financial condition. In the absence of the will, as per the Hindu

Succession Act, both sons would inherit equally.

Through a will, it is possible to allocate a particular property to one family member and ask that family member to pay a certain fixed amount per month towards pocket money, etc., to another family member. This concept is known as the concept of "annual charge". Creating annual charge through the process of a will is legal. For example, if the will is prepared, then it is possible for a person to allocate his property to his only son and ask him to make payment of Rs. 2,000 per month to his sister. The concept of annual charge cannot be implemented in the absence of a will.

Thus, a will is a useful document. Everyone should take advantage of the freedom and authority to dispose of his assets according his will. A will is a legal document. Apart from these advantages, preparation of a will envisages a lot of tax planning advantages which will become a reality in the family of the person inheriting the assets through a will. It is because of all these advantages, in particular, that persons generally above the age of 50 must prepare a will. However, there is no disadvantage at all in preparing a will in comparison with not preparing a will.

Thus, making a will will not only lead to a more efficient, easy and quick distribution of wealth of the deceased, thereby leaving little room for disputes, but will also prevent a person from undergoing lengthy and expensive legal procedures.

Drafting a Will

The first step in drafting a will is to make a list of all movable and immovable things belonging to the testator. This list will help in deciding which asset is to be given to which particular member of the family. The list will also ensure that no item is left out. The list can be further divided into categories, like highly valuable, valuable and less valuable or ABC category. The list of costly personal effects or items in category A should include items such as residential property, commercial property, machinery, show pieces, antiques as well as costly furniture, etc. Category B could have car/ shares/securities, etc. Category C can include TV, gadgets, jewellery, etc. The testator can categorize his valuables as he thinks fit.

The next step is to prepare a list of all persons to whom he wishes to give something. While preparing the list of all the beneficiaries, it is better to note down the full name as well as the father's name of the person, especially when there is a joint family. This is to ensure absolute clarity of his thoughts and avoid any confusion whatsoever, at the time of distribution.

Both the lists are very handy and will help to distribute the assets in the exact and correct names of different family members. The third step would be to decide and compile a final list which contains the assets item-wise and the name of the person who should get it.

Sometimes, the person preparing a will may desire to distribute the assets to selected family members, but he may also desire to distribute a token amount or a particular item to another person. He can then include the name of the person against the item or mention the amount to be given.

The testator should also make a checklist of all pending commitments. This chart would be a sort of ready reckoner of the testator's commitment to different family members, for which monetary funds are required. For example, if you still have one or two daughters to be married, then there is the responsibility of making provisions for their marriage. The checklist must also contain obligations that are to be fulfilled through the will. Likewise, if a son is unmarried, then some jewellery can be allocated to be given away to the daughter-in-law when she arrives. The commitment may also be with reference to permanent maintenance of some handicapped members of the family, for which you will like to make a provision in the will.

In this way, the total planning can be effectively done of all the assets of the testator. The checklists will ensure that, as far as possible, all matters are taken care of properly.

One should also prepare a list of the various liabilities as on the date of the execution of a will. The various liabilities which are yet to be discharged by the person preparing a will together with an action plan and the responsibility of specific family members to discharge these liabilities, must be listed. The person preparing the will can also pass on specific assets to a particular person together with liabilities attached to those assets. Sometimes, one asset may be inherited by the legal heirs together with certain liabilities which may be or may not be connected with the assets which are inherited. Hence, preparation of a chart of the various important liabilities is a prerequisite to writing a will.

A will requires the appointment of an executor for executing a will. It is now time to think and decide the name of the person whom you would like to nominate as an executor of the will. There can also be joint executors of a will. Similarly, the executor of a will can be a male person or a female person. If a female person is appointed as an executor, she is known as an executrix of the will. The powers, rights and duties of the executor is to distribute the assets of the testator, according to the specific directions as contained in the will. The executor should be an honest person and he should be concerned about the welfare of the family. There is no problem in appointing one of the beneficiaries of your assets as an executor. Thus a person who is likely to receive certain funds as per the will, may also be nominated separately as an executor to the will.

Another important aspect which should be taken into account while getting ready for executing a will is the witnesses to the will. There should be a minimum of two witnesses to a will. These two witnesses may be male or female. Identify two persons whom you feel you can request to be witnesses to the will. Also check on the availability of these witnesses at the time of execution/registration of the will.

It is a well-known fact that when the will is finally executed, both these witnesses must be ready to sign the will. Hence while you decide the names of the persons who can be requested to witness a will, make sure that they are easily available for signing as witnesses to your will. As far as possible, the witnesses to your will should not be interested parties or beneficiaries to your will.

The testator must also decide on the person who is going to write a will. For this purpose you can contact any civil lawyer or write down your will yourself. There is no specification of writing a will in a particular format or a particular language. Hence, it is easy to write a will. A family lawyer or any literate person can draft a will and he must keep your interest and sentiments in mind. Draft wills are found at the back of many legal books.

After this, the assets distribution plan can be got ready. For this purpose, it is necessary to think about personal attachments to different members of the family and the desire to distribute the assets to such family members. It is the sole discretion of the testator to distribute assets through a will to the family members, as he pleases. It is possible to think and decide on the various emotional aspects that are to be a part of the will.

Drafting and preparation of a will is a very emotional matter and to achieve the best results of effective and proper drafting of the will, it is better that the person gets ready with all preliminary details mentioned above, and then proceeds to draft the will.

Writing a Will

A will, as mentioned earlier, can be written on plain paper. A will can be written by hand or it can be typed on a manual typewriter, or on the computer. It should be very clearly and neatly written so as to express the intentions of the person preparing the will. Since the contents of a will can take effect only when the testator dies, it is not possible to clarify what is written. Hence utmost care has to be taken to ensure that the will is crystal clear, with no ambiguity, and the desires and the intentions are clearly spelt out so that no double meanings can be derived while reading the will. A will alone will be the guiding factor in disposing the testator's assets. There may be a repetition of a particular sentiment or a particular emotion or desire of the testator. Repetitions itself will not cause any problems about the legality or validity of the will. However, care has to be taken to ensure that the repetition does not cause confusion or doubt, but only clarifies a point further.

If the testator intends to register a will, he should leave sufficient space for pasting a photograph on top of the first page. The first paragraph of a will should contain the name of the person preparing the will, age, father/husband's name, religion, occupation, as well as mailing address. The first preamble to a will should contain the date of preparation of the will. In the first paragraph itself it should be mentioned that the present will is the last and final will, revoking all previous wills which had been prepared. There should also be a clear-cut mention in a will that it is prepared without any persuasion or coercion, and out of free will only.

In the next paragraph, it is better if a mention is made that the person preparing the will 'hereby revokes all the former wills and codicils made by him or her'. This can be done in case a person has prepared a will earlier and this is the revised will. In such a case, the details must be clearly written and also the date of the preparation of the earlier will. In case the previous will was registered, it is better to give reference about the same in the new will, namely, the date of registration of the previous will.

The next paragraph should contain the name of the person who is appointed as the sole executor of the will, along with a brief description, i.e. Mr— —S/o— — — Aged— — —who is my nephew, etc. While writing the name of the executor of the will, mention can be made of the name of the father/ husband of the executor, as well as the mailing address. This is to avoid ambiguity. It is possible for a person to appoint one single executor to a will, or there can be joint executors. This paragraph then should contain the names and details of both the executors to the will. In the case of joint executors, both of them share equal powers with reference to a will. In the event of the executor predeceasing the testator of a will, there is a necessity of providing another executor to the will. To avoid this problem, it is better that in a will the name of the executor is mentioned. A second executor should be named and it should be clarified that in the event that the first executor expires before the death of the testator, the new executor would execute the will. When the name of the executor is clearly spelt out in the will, all problems of handling the estate of the person preparing the will is solved.

It is better if a will mention's the various powers which are to be enjoyed by the executor of the estate. Likewise, rights, duties and obligations of the executor should be clearly spelt out. There should be a mention that after the demise of the testator, the executor will have power to open a bank account. Powers of the executor may be further clarified with regard to handling of the assets of the testator. From a practical angle, it is important that powers be showered on the executors, in the interest of the beneficiaries, to invest in movable and immovable assets in the manner as he would deem it fit. If a person finds difficulty in writing the detailed powers, rights, duties and obligations of the executor in a will, then it would suffice if a mention is just made that "the executor will have all the powers under the law which are necessary for proper management of the assets and distribution of the assets to all the beneficiaries mentioned in the will".

The executor will be in charge of the entire estate after the demise of the testator or author of the will. The executor will have all the powers under the law to implement the directions regarding the bequests as also for the administration of the estate in accordance with the provisions of this will. Without prejudice to the generality of the foregoing, the executor will, inter-alia, have the following powers:

a) To open an account with any bank or banks or post office, to operate such an account and to give instructions to the bank or post office, and to provide for the opening and operation of such an account by any one or more of the agent/agents or constituted attorney appointed by the executor.

b) To accept any gift, donation or contribution for the benefit of the estate, in cash or kind.

c) To invest and keep invested the property comprised in the estate or the income thereof, in immovable or movable property or in any deposit with or loans to any company, bank, firm or any other person, and to alter, vary or transpose such investments from time to time, as may not be required to be distributed in specie to any legates, as he may in his discretion think fit, for others of the name or alike or different nature.

d) To let out or demise any immovable property comprised in the estate for such period and for such rent and on such terms and conditions, as he may in his discretion think fit.

e) To borrow or receive or secure payment of money and also to lend money comprised in the estate either with or without security.

f) To adjust, settle, compromise, compound, refer to arbitration of all actions, suits and proceedings relating to the estate.

g) To appoint constituted attorneys or agents, and to delegate such attorneys or agents all or any of the powers vested in him under this will, and from time to time, remove such attorneys or agents and to appoint others in his or their place.

h) To carry on any activity which may be incidental to the exercise of his duties and powers under this will.

The next part of a will should have broad details of assets as they are, on the date of preparation of the will. It is not compulsory to write down all the assets possessed by a person as they are, on the date of the will. However, it would be better if broad details of the assets owned by a person are clearly spelt out in the will itself. For example, if there are shares and debentures, let us say of fifty companies, the testator may not write the names of all the fifty companies in which he possesses shares; but for the purpose of the will, it would suffice to write down in the list of assets, e.g., "I am in possession of shares and debentures of various companies. The shares/debentures are to be equally distributed among my nephews and nieces...". While writing down the list of the main assets in a will, the details of movable properties in particular, should be clearly spelt out. If the person preparing the will is not the sole owner of a particular property, but is the owner of a certain percentage of the property, then there should be a clear-cut mention of the same in the will. While mentioning the details of the assets in a will as they are on the date of preparation of a will, one need not be too meticulous about writing down the exact amount. It would suffice if mention is made of all the assets like, "I own National Saving Certificates, Bank Fixed Deposits, Units of the UTI, etc." It would also be better if a mention is made in the asset's list about the various LIC policies which had been taken by the person preparing the will, so that through the will, the maturity amount in respect of insurance can be suitably transferred to the legal heirs in the manner as the testator of the will desires.

The next step in writing a will relates to the distribution of the movable as well as immovable assets amongst different members of the family. In this paragraph, various assets should be mentioned which are allocated to different individual members in the family. Likewise, if certain funds are demarcated for being given to charitable trusts or institutions, they should also find a specific mention in the will. From the point of view of practical simplification, it would be better if the assets are clearly distributed amongst different persons. However, it is possible for the person preparing the will to mention the percentage of distribution of the assets out of the total assets in favour of different persons. Let us assume that a person has cash, a bank balance, a house, property, a plot of land, shares and fixed deposits. One way of distributing the assets could be that the cash and bank balance are allocated to the wife, while the land is allotted to a daughter, and the building is allotted to the son. On the other hand, if the person creating a will would have desired that the assets are to be distributed in the name of the different family members as a percentage of the total value of the assets, then the legal requirements for the proper drafting of a will would have been fulfilled even though in the will he may have just mentioned the requisite percentage of ownership of the total estate. For example, if in the will it is mentioned that as on the date of his death, 60% of all his assets would go to his wife, 30% to his son and 10% to his daughter, such a distribution would also be deemed valid. However, it is always better to clearly demarcate the movable as well as immovable assets amongst different family members in specific shares. The costly personal effects like television sets, music systems, antiques, paintings, cameras, carpets, etc., should also be clearly distributed to different persons. Although in most cases, in comparison with the total stake of a person, these personal effects in monetary terms do not mean valuable assets as far as the market price is concerned, yet distribution of these assets has a great emotional and sentimental attachment and value. For example, some of the small items like some paintings or antiques which had always been very dear to the daughter and the person would specifically like these items to be given away to her for emotional reasons, it would be better if in the will it is clearly written that these assets should be given away to the daughter.

A will should also contain details with regard to payment of liabilities, loans and advances of the person preparing the will. Generally, it will suffice to write in the will that after the demise of the person preparing the will, first of all, all liabilities will be paid from the estate and then the balance amount will be divided amongst the beneficiaries as mentioned in the will. Similarly, it is possible for the person preparing the will, to specifically mention that certain liabilities will go to specific persons who are his legal heirs.

When a will is prepared by a person who is illiterate, then apart from the above mentioned formalities to be complied with for the purpose of writing a will, it should be mentioned on the last page of the will that it has been read over and explained to the person executing the will. The person reading and explaining the will has also to sign on the will. Generally speaking, one of the witnesses to a will writes on the last page that he has read out the will to the author and explained to him/her the contents of the will.

After taking care of the above mentioned points, the task of writing the will is almost complete. At the end of the will, it should be mentioned by the person preparing the will, that after his death the income tax, wealth tax and other tax liabilities and taxes, if any, will be first paid out of his estate. It is also better if it is mentioned that "if the estate of the person preparing the will is insufficient to meet any of the bequests, legacies, etc., then the amount earmarked for different bequests and legacies, etc., shall abate proportionately".

Besides, if a person desires to write certain emotional matters concerning his liking or disliking about the members of his family, or appreciating the nature of work of some family members, he can do so.

It is just his personal choice to write all these general things. The number of pages in a will depends upon the total subject matter contained therein. A normal will can just be written in one or two pages, while a big exhaustive will may contain ten to fifteen pages.

Registration of a Will

It has been mentioned earlier that registration of a will is not compulsory. The question of legal validity of a will does not make any distinction between a registered will or an unregistered will. Registration of a will has to be done in the office of the sub-registrar, i.e., the place where we normally go and register our property-related documents, etc. The expenses involved in the registration of a will at the office of a sub-registrar are very minimal.

Normally, the total expenditure involved in the registration of a will varies between Rs. 100 to Rs. 200 only. It would be pertinent to note that the registration charges for registering the will in the office of the registrar/sub-registrar do not vary according to the value of the assets mentioned in the will. Thus, fixed registration charges are payable for the registration of a will.

From a practical angle, it is advisable that one day prior to the date when you want to register your will, you should go to the office of the sub-registrar and inquire about any other formality required for the purpose of registration. In different states, the office of the sub-registrar might impose a particular compliance-formality for the registration of a will. This should be inquired into a day prior to the registration of the will so that on the day of registration, there is no problem and the registration takes place smoothly. Generally, for the purpose of the registration of a will, in addition to the original will, one extra copy of the will has to be signed by the person making the will. For the purpose of the registration of a will there should be at least two witnesses to the will. These two witnesses should sign only on the last page of the will and not on every page of the will. For the purpose of registration, the author of a will or the testator is required to give documentary evidence regarding his identification. Normally, for this purpose, a copy of the voter's card or passport would be sufficient to prove the identity of the person executing the will. A xerox copy of the voter's card/identity card or the passport must be attached with the will at the time of registration. Two photographs of the executor of the will are also required for the purpose of registration. One photograph should be pasted on the original will while the second copy of the photograph should be pasted on the duplicate or the xerox copy of the will. Care should be taken to see that the photograph is not stapled but is pasted on the first page of the will.

As the photograph is required to be pasted on the first page of the will, it is suggested that the will be typed after leaving sufficient space on the top of the first page for affixing the photograph. The photographs of witnesses to the will are not required to be affixed. The witnesses to the will are also required to carry their identity cards. The identity card can be either a voter's card or a passport. The witnesses should also enclose a xerox copy of their identity card/ passport with the will. In many places, the sub-registrar may just note down the identity card number or passport number, in which case, the copy of the identity card/ passport need not be attached with the will. As soon as the will is signed on every page by the testator of the will, or the author of the will, and also signed by two witnesses to the will, then the will is ready for being presented to the sub-registrar for the purpose of registration. Once signatures, etc., have been done on the will, it would be registered by the office of the sub-registrar. A small receipt, evidencing the registration of the will, will be given to the person preparing his will. On production of this small receipt, generally after three weeks or so, the original will, duly registered, will be returned. The will can be collected by any person after producing the said receipt which was issued by the office of the sub-registrar. It is not necessary for the author of the will to be personally present to collect the original will.

Sometimes, it may so happen that the person preparing the will is not in good health, or is hospitalized, or is unable to move to the office of the sub-registrar for the purpose of registration. In such cases, the sub-registrar can be requested to register the will either in the hospital or at the residence or office of the person executing the will. This is known as calling the sub-registrar on "commission". A small fee for this purpose has to be paid in the sub-registrar's office. Sometimes for the purpose of "commission" the office of the sub-registrar may even ask for a medical certificate of the person preparing the will. Thus, registration of the will in the office of the sub-registrar is a very simple affair and it does not take a long time. No stamp paper is required even in respect of a will which is registered in the office of the sub-registrar. Plain paper will suffice. The will to be registered can be written in any language. This will can be written by hand, it can be typed on a manual typewriter, electronic typewriter or on a computer. The legal validity of a will is the same in all situations. When a will is written by hand, the same can be written by the person who is preparing his will, or it can also be written by some other person for and on behalf of the person signing the will.

Thumb impressions of the person preparing the will and also those of the witnesses are required on the will.

The registration of a will can also be done by registering it with a notary public. A notary public is so appointed by the government. He generally sits outside any court or in any good commercial locality. He charges a very nominal fee for authentication. When a will is registered before the notary public, the said will should be signed on all pages by the person preparing the will. Both the witnesses should also sign the will. Thereafter, the notary public will affix his rubber stamp and notarial ticket on the will. As mentioned earlier, the legal impact of the will is the same whether it is registered or unregistered. However, it may again be noted that it is always better to register a will. This is because when a will is lost or defaced, a certified copy thereof can be obtained from the sub-registrar's office. We have seen that the registration can either be done in the office of the sub-registrar or before the notary public. However, if the choice is there, then it is better to register it in the office of the sub-registrar.

If a will has been registered in the office of the sub-registrar and is required to be changed at a later date, then reference should be mentioned in the current will about the details pertaining to the registration and cancellation of the earlier will.

The Role of the Executor

An executor has the greatest role to play in the final execution of a will. Although he generally does not sign the will, after the death of the testator, it is this man who has to undertake the duty of executing the wishes and desires of the person who has nominated him as the executor of his will. The duties of the executor are related to the collection of all the assets and debts of the deceased person, payment of all the debts and finally, the distribution of the estate of the deceased person according to the will. Whenever a probate (i.e., the certified copy of the will granted by a court) is to be obtained, the same will be granted by the court on an application by the executor. If the executor desires and deems fit, he can distribute the assets of the deceased person in terms of a will either in one go or in instalments depending on the circumstances. Sometimes a minor is also appointed as an executor. Legally, it is possible to appoint the minor as an executor, but during the period he is a minor, he cannot administer the terms and conditions as mentioned in a will. If there is more than one executor as in joint executors, they are regarded as one person and have to exercise their duties jointly. In the case of more than one executor, the death of one executor will mean that the rights and powers of the executor are going to be vested with another sole executor.

For all practical purposes, the executor of a will is actually the legal representative of the deceased. The executor is also required to do other acts for and on behalf of the deceased person, i.e., if the income tax return is to be filed, the same will be signed by the executor on behalf of the testator. The role of the executor is to execute a will. He has no right to enjoy or use any of the assets of the deceased unless he inherits it.

His duty is the distribution of these assets amongst the legal heirs of the deceased in the ratio as mentioned in the will. It may also be the duty of the executor to dispose of the body of the testator. Thereafter, he should proceed with ascertaining the assets of the deceased, taking account of all assets, compile the list of all the assets, and thereafter make payment of the legitimate dues, government dues and other dues of the deceased person, to arrive at the net value of the estate and then proceed to obtain the probate and finally distribute the assets. It may be noted here that the executor does not have the power to distribute the assets in the manner he deems fit or in the manner required, depending on the circumstances and the family of the testator, because all along, the executor has to exercise his rights of distribution of the assets exactly accordingly to the will. Thus, his duties are to distribute assets as per the directions contained in a will. The duties of the executor will continue till such time that the complete distribution of the assets takes place. There is no specific period during which he has to complete the work of the final distribution of the assets. The period will, however, depend upon the facts and circumstances of a particular case. The legal heirs, as per a will, cannot force upon the executor to speed up the distribution work. The executor generally would not be receiving salary or remuneration for carrying out the duties as an executor. However, he is entitled to receive reimbursement of the expenses actually incurred by him in the execution of the will. The will of a person may also provide for payment of a particular remuneration for the executor during the period the execution has not been completed, or provide for a payment of a lump sum amount to the executor towards his services for implementation of the will. If this amount is mentioned in the will, the same will have to be paid to the executor before actual distribution of the assets to the legal representative, as mentioned in the will. If, however, no mention is made in the will regarding payment of any remuneration to the executor, then nothing will be payable to the executor for his services rendered.

The executor is advised to prepare a statement, preferably in the form of an affidavit, about the performance of his various duties in connection with a will. A specimen draft of such an affidavit is given below:

"Draft of an Affidavit by an Executor for the creation of Trust under will, and distribution of assets of the Testator among legatees as per Will:

AFFIDAVIT

I, ABC, son of DEF, by faith Hindu, by occupation businessman/service holder, residing at ...., do hereby solemnly affirm and declare as follows:

1. My father Late GHI made a will on _____ (date) which was registered

with the Registrar of Assurances, _____ (place) on _______ (date) vide Book No. _______ pages _______ being No. ________ of ________. He expired on __________ (date of death). I have been appointed as an executor of the said Will.

2. Under the said Will, the Late ______________ (Name of Testator) created a family trust to be operative after his demise only. I am also one of the Trustees under the said Will for the Trust. The relevant extracts from the said Will in respect of the creation of the Trust, description of the trust, trustees, beneficiaries, amount settled on trust, etc. are given below:

"(Herein give the actual extract of the relevant clauses of the Will)"

3. According to the directions contained in Clause No. ________ of the said Will, I, as executor, distributed on ______ (date of distribution) Rs.______ cash to the trustees of the said Trust, viz. ______ (name of the Trust declared under Will).

4. In accordance with Clause No. _____ of the said Will I have handed over Rs. ______ cash and ornaments weighting approx. ______ gms. to the trustees (including myself) of the said Trust on ______ (date of handing

over) and to the legatees as given below as a part of the distribution of the net estate of Late __________ (name of the Testator). The said gold ornaments and cash since then are being held as the property under the aforesaid Trust and by the individual legatees as mentioned below:

Name of Legatee	**Amount Rs.**
i. Shri R	________
ii. Shri S	________
iii. Smt. T	________
iv. Master U through father and natural guardian Shri W	________

v. ______ (and so on) ______

Total ______

5. The above statements are made for the sake of clarity and record.
6. The above statements are true to the best of my knowledge and belief.

Solemnly declared and affirmed

before me by Shri ______ (executor)

at New Delhi on______

Identified by me and signed in my presence

____

Before me

Notary Public "

The liability of the executor is limited only to the extent of the estate which he is controlling. Under no circumstances can the liability of the executor be extended beyond the amount which he has received for the distribution in terms of a will. However, the executor must diligently take care of all the investments, disposal of the assets, etc.

As regards the provisions relating to the executors of a will, reference may be made to sections 168 and 169 of the Income tax Act, 1961, as reproduced below:

Executors

Section 168

1) Subject as hereinafter provided, the income of the estate of a deceased person shall be chargeable to tax in the hands of the executor –

   a) if there is only one executor, then, as if the executor were an individual; or

   b) if there are more executors than one, then, as if the executors were an association of persons;

and for the purposes of this Act, the executor shall be deemed to be resident or non-resident, according as the deceased person was a resident or non-resident during the previous year in which his death took place.

2. The assessment of an executor under this section shall be made separately from any assessment that may be made on him in respect of his own income.

3. Separate assessments shall be made under this section on the total income of each completed previous year or part thereof as is included in the period from the date of the death to the date of complete distribution to the beneficiaries of the estate

according to their several interests.

4. In computing the total income of any previous year under this section, any income of the estate of that previous year distributed to, or applied to the benefit of, any specific legatee of the estate during that previous year shall be excluded; but the income so excluded shall be included in the total income of the previous year of such specific legatee.

Explanation – In this section, "executor" includes an administrator or the person administering the estate of a deceased person.

Right of an executor to recover tax paid Section 169

The provisions of section 162 shall, so far as may be, apply in the case of an executor in respect of tax paid or payable by him as they apply in the case of a representative assessee.

The Role of a Will in Tax Savings

There are various tax advantages, other than the creation of a discretionary trust through a will, which can be secured for the members of the family of the taxpayer, through a will only. For example, a separate income tax file for a Hindu Undivided Family can be established by a transfer of property through a will. Similarly, bequests can be made to minor sons and minor grandsons through a will in a manner that there is no clubbing of income under the provision of section 64 of the IT Act. Transfer of assets without any consideration can be made by a will to one's wife or one's daughter-in-law, without attracting the clubbing provisions of section 64 (1) of the IT Act. Another important tax advantage of a will is to secure an annual charge on property particularly for the benefit of daughters. This can easily be done through a will. Where a person is interested in the creation of a charitable trust or the transfer of property after his demise, for the benefit of the public for charitable purposes, the same can easily be done by means of a charitable trust. The property belonging to the testator, can be enjoyed by him with absolute powers during his lifetime and its disposition can be arranged as per his desire, through proper declaration in a will. In this chapter, the different tax planning aspects through a will have been described in detail.

Having seen the general provision of making a valid will, we are in a position to examine some of the important tax planning aspects of a will. One of the important means of tax planning to be adopted through a will is the creation of a Hindu

Undivided Family. Under the provisions of section 64(2), where a member of the Hindu family impresses his self-acquired property with the character of a joint family property, the income therefrom is to be clubbed with his income. This disadvantage can be overcome by proper tax planning and transfer of certain properties in favour of the coparcenary of a Hindu governed by the Mitakshara school of Hindu Law, so that a separate Hindu Undivided Family comes into existence which can be recognized as an independent and separate taxable entity under the income tax law.

There are various schools of Hindu Law. However, strictly speaking, there are only two schools – the Dayabhaga and the Mitakshra. Other schools like the Dravida, the Mithila, the Benares and the Maharashtra schools are really the sub-schools of the Mitakshra. They differ from one another only in minor matters. However, there are differences of fundamental characters between the Mitakshra and the Dayabhaga.

The main points of difference between the Mitakshra and the Dayabhaga (Hindu Law) as per

Raghavachariar's Hindu Law are tabulated in the table given below:

The Mitakshra School	The Dayabhaga School
1. The son gets a right by birth in the joint family property and can insist on a partition even during his father's lifetime.	1. There is no right by birth accorded to a son and he cannot demand partition so long as the father is alive.
2. The son by virtue to his right by birth can restrain unauthorised alienations of ancestral property by the father.	2. The father is the absolute owner of the properties and can deal with the property in any way he likes.

3. There is no absolute right for a collateral member of the joint family, like a brother, to alienate his share in the joint family property; and on his death, without a male issue, his interest survives to his brother.	3. Owing to the existence of the theory of quasi-severalty each brother can alienate his interest, and on his death, without a male issue, his interest descends to his widow.
4. The widow of a deceased coparcener cannot enforce partition of her husband's share against his brothers' wishes.	4. The widow becomes a coparcener with her husband's brothers and can insist on a partition of his share.

5. Rule of propinquity is the dominating rule of preference in succession.	5. Test of religious efficacy is the prevailing rule.

For example, an old father, Mr. 'F' aged 82 years, wishes to transfer certain property to his son 'S' and his wife and children. He could make a will and transfer the property to the Hindu Undivided Family of his son 'S' in unequivocal terms, that the property transferred belongs to the Hindu Undivided Family of 'S' only and not to individual members thereof. On the demise of the testator, the property bequeathed to the Hindu Undivided Family in the above case would belong to the separate entity of the HUF only. This Hindu Undivided Family would be able to enjoy the separate exemption limit applicable to it under the Finance Act, for the time being in force.

Under the provisions of section 64 (1), if a person makes a gift to his minor children, minor grandchildren (paternal side), then the income accruing or arising to the minor children/minor grandchildren (other than disabled children), would be clubbed with the income of the father or mother. This would not, however, be the case if a bequest is made to minor children or minor grandchildren of the testator through a will. The reason is obvious. After the demise of the testator, the question of clubbing the income of the minor children/grandchildren with the income of the testator would not arise. Hence, a will can be adopted as a proper device for transfer of property by way of bequest through will so as to result in a lot of tax saving.

During the life of a taxpayer, any gift made by him to his wife or vice versa, would be liable to be included in the income of the donor under the provisions of section 64 (1). Hence, bequests can be made of the property to the extent considered necessary, in favour of the testator's wife so as to make the testator's wife a separate taxable entity, if she is not already so. This can help in a lot of tax saving for the wife. With the abolition of the estate duty, this device as well as the other modes of transfer of property by tax planning through wills can be adopted.

Sections 64 (1) (vi) and (viii) provides that where a transfer is made in favour of the daughter-in-law, either directly or for her benefit to the trustees of a trust, the income from the transferred assets would be clubbed with the income of the donor. Hence, during one's lifetime, it is not possible to make gifts in favour of the daughter-in-law or through the medium of a trust to the daughter-in-law. This handicap can, however, be overcome by tax planning through a will. Thus, a bequest can be made in favour of the daughter-in-law, so as to confer an absolute title to the daughter-in-law, and make her a taxable entity, if she is not already one, after the testator's demise. There should not be any clubbing of the income of the daughter-in-law with the income of the executor of the estate of the deceased person after the testator's death.

Through a will a discretionary trust can be created which could be charged to tax at normal rates. It is provided in clause (ii) of the first proviso to section 164 (1), that if there is only one trust declared by a will, then the income of the discretionary trust would be chargeable to income tax as if it were the total income of an individual. Make sure only one discretionary trust is created through the will.

A discretionary trust is normally liable to income tax at the maximum marginal rate of tax as per section 164(1) of the Income tax Act, 1961, but there are four specific exceptions to this provision, as contained in the first proviso to section 164(1). For a ready reference, the full extract of section 164(1) and the first proviso thereto, are reproduced below.

"Section 164(1)

Subject to the provisions of sub-sections (2) and (3), where any income in respect of which the persons mentioned in clauses (iii) and (iv) of sub-section (1) of section 160, are liable as representative assessees or any part thereof is not specifically receivable on behalf or for the benefit of any one person or where the individual shares of the persons on whose behalf or for whose benefit such income or such part thereof is receivable are indeterminate or unknown (such income, such part of the income and such persons being hereafter in this section referred to as "relevant income", "part of relevant income" and "beneficiaries", respectively), tax shall be charged on the relevant income or part of relevant income at the maximum marginal rate—

Provided that in a case where:

i) none of the beneficiaries has any other income chargeable under this Act exceeding the maximum amount not chargeable to tax in the case of an association of persons or is a beneficiary under any other trust; or

ii) the relevant income or part of the relevant income is receivable under a trust declared by any person under will and such trust is the only trust so declared by him; or

iii) the relevant income or part of the relevant income is receivable under a trust created before the

1st day of March, 1970, by a non-testamentary instrument and the Assessing Officer is satisfied, having regard to all the circumstances existing at the relevant time, that the trust was created bona fide exclusively for the benefit of the relatives of the settlor, or where the settlor is a Hindu Undivided Family, exclusively for the benefit of the member of such a family, in circumstances where such relatives or members were mainly dependent on the settlor for their support and maintenance; or

iv) the relevant income is receivable by the trustees on behalf of a provident fund, superannuation fund, gratuity fund, pension fund or any other fund created bona fide by a person carrying on a business or profession exclusively for the benefit of persons employed in such business or profession,

tax shall be charged on the relevant income or part of the relevant income as if it were the total income of an association of persons."

After the death of an individual, the income from the estate of the testator or deceased person is chargeable in the hands of the executor or executors, if any, under the provisions of section 168 of the Income tax Act, 1961. The expression "executor" includes an administrator or other person administering the estate of a deceased person. A person in de facto management of the property of the deceased who dies intestate is also assessable as executor under section 168. Where a person leaves a will, a person or persons administering the estate of the deceased person is, or are, thus known as the executor or executors. Where the estate is administered by a lady, she is known as executrix.

Where a person dies having made a will in which some specific property is to be given or distributed to certain specific beneficiaries or legatees, the work of the executor includes, inter alia, the distribution of application of the money or income of the estate for the benefit of the specific legatee or legatees or beneficiaries.

Thus, there can be separate assessments in respect of the income of the estate of a deceased person in the hands of the executor, specific legatees or the trustees of a trust declared by a will and a lot of income tax can be saved through the application of the provisions of the

Income tax law. The amount of income tax saving in this regard, through proper tax planning, is really immense.

The saving of income tax through application of the provisions of the Income tax Act, 1961 by proper drafting of the will is illustrated in this example. Supposing Mr. 'A' has a gross rental income of Rs. 80,000 per annum. Besides, he owns fixed deposits worth Rs. 6 lakhs in different banks on which he gets interest @ 10% p.a. He has invested Rs. 5 lakhs in fixed deposits with certain good companies on which he gets a net interest of 12% per annum, i.e., Rs. 60,000 p.a. For the financial year 2001-2002, i.e., relevant to the assessment year 2002-2003, he would be required to pay income tax on the income from all these sources. His total income would be computed as under:

Income from house property:	
Gross rental value:	Rs. 80,000
(Question of house-tax is not considered here).	
Less: Deduction in respect of repairs, etc., at 30% of the annual value of Rs. 80,000:	Rs. 24,000
Net Income from house property:	Rs. 56,000

Income from other sources:	
(a) Interest on bank fixed deposit receipts ... Rs. 60,000	
(b) Interest on fixed deposits with companies @ 12% on Rs. 5,00,000 ...Rs. 60,000	Rs. 1,20,000
	Rs. 1,76,000
Gross Total Income:	Rs. 1,76,000
Less: Deduction in respect of interest on bank fixed deposits under section 80L (Maximum Rs. 9,000)	Rs. 9,000
Total Income	Rs. 1,67,000
Income tax payable (by not considering the effect of 2% surcharge)	Rs. 24,100

Supposing 'A' were to make a will and die on 1.4.2001 the income tax saving as per the various clauses in the will drafted by him, is shown below:

Mr. A has given the property to his wife Mrs. A who has no other income. Mr. A gives the bank fixed deposits worth Rs. 6 lakhs to a discretionary trust declared in the will for the benefit of the sons, daughters and future grandsons and grand-daughters of 'A'. He makes bequest for the children of his second son, 'C' through which various fixed deposits with the various companies worth Rs. 5 lakhs are given to them. In this case, as A dies on 1.4.2001, for the financial year 2001-2002, relevant to the assessment year 2002-2003, the net taxable income from house property in the hands of Mrs. A would be Rs. 56,000 only. She has no other income liable to income tax. She will be required to pay tax only on Rs. 56,000 which would be Rs. 600 only. In the case of a discretionary trust, the net income from interest on bank fixed deposits would be 10% of Rs. 6 lakhs, i.e. Rs. 60,000. The trust would be liable at the rate applicable to associations of persons, i.e. on the total income as per section 164 of the Income tax Act. Thus, Rs. 50,000 out of Rs. 60,000 bank interest would be fully exempt. The next Rs. 10,000 would be liable to income tax at 10% so the trustees of the discretionary trust for the assessment year 2002-2003 would be required to tax of Rs. 1,000 only. As regards the legatees being the children of his son C on the supposition that the fixed deposit receipts are not distributed and they remain in the estate, the executor will be liable to tax as an individual under section 168. Thus, the income of Rs. 60,000 being the 12% of Rs. 5 lakhs would be assessable in the hands of the executor as an individual and thus, he would be liable to income tax only of Rs. 1,000. Thus, on the death of A on 1.4.2001, the total tax payable by Mrs. A, the trustees of the discretionary trust and the executor on the entire estate left by A, would be Rs. 600 + Rs. 1,000 + Rs. 1,000 = Rs. 2,600 only, as against the tax which otherwise would have been payable by A had A not died and not made a will, viz., of Rs. 24,100. Thus, there would be a net income tax saving of Rs. 21,500 (Rs. 24,100 less Rs. 2,600), through proper drafting of the will.

From the above description of the various aspects of wills, it is clear that a considerable amount of tax saving can be achieved through judicious drafting of a will. The proverb "Where there is a will, there is a way" can be altered to "Where there is a will, there is a tax saving." As the assessment of an executor has to be made separately from any other assessment that may be made on him in respect of his own income, there is no risk of extra income tax or any other income tax burden if the executor were not to complete the distribution or application of the income of the estate of the deceased for a long period. It is possible in many instances, to administer the estate after distribution to certain specific legatees so that the estate is assessed to a separate income tax assessment through the executor. Thus, there could be several assessments in respect of the income of the estate left behind by a deceased person. For example, a discretionary trust created by a will declared by the deceased would be separately assessable to the income tax and would be chargeable to normal rates of income tax applicable to an individual under the provisions of the first proviso to section 164 (1). Similarly, where specific portion of the estate is distributed to certain beneficiaries who have no other income or who have income below the taxable limit, it would be possible to have separate assessment of the different beneficiaries in a manner so as to attract "nil" or the least income tax. After the distribution of the income from the estate or application thereof for the benefit of the specific legatees of the estate and handing over the particular sum earmarked for the trust to the trustees, the income from the balance estate left by the deceased person would be assessable to income tax in a separate assessment in the hands of the executor, leading to a good deal of income tax saving through proper tax planning. Similar benefits are also available under the Wealth tax Act as well.

The savings in wealth tax through proper drafting of the will, is explained in this illustration. Supposing Mrs. 'X' is the owner of jewellery worth Rs. 50 lakhs as on 31.3.2001. She has no other asset or property. She would be liable to pay wealth tax on Rs. 50 lakhs, less the exemption limit of Rs. 15 lakhs, i.e. on Rs. 35 lakhs at 1%, namely Rs. 35,000. Mrs. X has made a will whereby she bequeaths Rs. 14 lakhs worth of jewellery to her husband who has no other taxable wealth. She bequeaths Rs. 13 lakhs worth of jewellery to her daughter-in-law, Mrs. A, who has also no taxable wealth with her. Likewise, she makes another bequest of Rs. 12 lakhs worth of jewellery to Mrs. B, her other daughter-in-law, who has also no other taxable wealth. The balance of Rs. 11 lakhs is put by her in a discretionary trust for the benefit of the sons, daughters, and future children of her sons A and B. Supposing, Mrs. X were to die on 1.4.2001, leaving Rs. 50 lakhs worth of jewellery and a will with the bequests as mentioned above, then the husband will be considered to be the owner of the jewellery worth of

Rs. 14 lakhs for the purposes of wealth tax. However, as he has no other taxable wealth, he will not be liable to any wealth tax. The net wealth would be below Rs. 15 lakhs. Likewise, Mrs. A and Mrs. B would also not be liable to any wealth tax on Rs. 13 lakhs and Rs. 12 lakhs respectively, received by them through the will, because they have no other taxable wealth. The discretionary trust will be liable to wealth tax only on Rs. 11 lakhs worth of the jewellery, but as this is below Rs. 15 lakhs, there is no liability to wealth tax. Further, the trust is also not liable to any wealth tax at all. In this illustration, it is assumed that the valuation of the jewellery as on 31.3.2001 and 31.3.2003 remains the same. Thus, no wealth tax would be payable by the legatees and the trustees on the jewellery received by them through the will of Mrs. X on her death. Though Mrs. X was liable to pay wealth tax of Rs. 35,000, there would be a saving of this sum on her death, through proper drafting of the will, as mentioned above.

The Role of Specific Legatees in a Will

When a will is prepared, it is possible that the testator to the will provided for specific amounts to be paid to a specific legatee. The legatees may be individuals, male or female, minor or major. Even a charitable trust, a religious trust, HUF, could be a legatee.

Persons who are unascertained (explained below) as on the date of preparation of a will can become a party to enjoy the bequest out of a will. For example, if the will provides for Rs. 10,000 to be paid to the wife of the grandson, assuming the grandson is still unmarried, then the sum of Rs. 10,000 will definitely have to be paid to the wife of the grandson when she comes. Similarly, if the bequest amount is to be paid to an unborn person, the same would also be legally valid. The amount to be given to various legacies through a will must be fully ascertained so that there is certainty with regard to the amount to be given away to a particular legatee. A specific legatee as mentioned in a will does not have much role to play. These legatees in the will would enjoy the amount of the assets as are specifically mentioned and meant for each of them. Besides, there may be certain conditions affixed in the will for each of the legatees or for some of the legatees. For example, Mr. 'A' bequests Rs. 20,000 through his will to his grandson Mst. 'B' when he attains the age of 21 years. Now as per the will, the legatee in the form of a minor child 'B' will get the money only when he is 21 years of age. This type of restriction can be put by the testator to the will. Similarly, a certain amount may be mentioned in the will to be payable to the specified legatee only after marriage. Putting up such types of conditions through the will would be perfectly legal. However, if a condition is mentioned in a will, the same will have to be complied with by the legatee to entitle the person of the funds or assets as mentioned in the will. Non-compliance of the specific condition mentioned in the will would disentitle the legatee from receiving the money.

If a beneficiary expires before the testator, then a will cannot be implemented in respect of the deceased because the legatee in such circumstances does not acquire any right to the property in the will, because the will comes into operation only after the death of the testator. However, if the legatee expires after the death of the testator but before the distribution of the amount earmarked for him, then his legal heirs would step into his shoes.

Where an amount is earmarked for a family trust or charity trust, then the trust continues to enjoy the amount earmarked in the will, because a trust does not die and hence the amount towards it does not lapse. A question sometimes arises as to whether a body corporate can become a legatee. The answer to this is in the affirmative. The body corporate or the partnership firm can also become a legatee. From the point of view of effective planning of the assets through a will and successful succession of the assets of the testator, it is recommended that the specific legatees are clearly spelt out in a will, so that the amount earmarked for each legatee can be given away by the executor.

The income tax saving through specific allotment of certain assets and income to a specific legatee is explained by means of an example. Supposing Mrs. D makes a will and distributes her only asset, namely,

Rs. 15 lakhs worth of fixed deposit receipts with various companies on which she gets an interest of 10% per annum. Her total income would be Rs. 1,50,000 on which she would normally be required to pay income tax of Rs. 19,000. She makes a will and allots Rs. 5 lakhs worth of fixed deposit receipts to each of her three granddaughters, Ms. A, Ms. B and Ms. C aged 21, 20 and 19. They are studying and they do not have any other income. Unfortunately, Mrs. D dies on 1.4.2001. As per the will, made by her, Rs. 5 lakhs worth of fixed deposit receipts would go to each of the specified legatees Ms. A,

Ms. B and Ms. C. The income received by them from the fixed deposit receipts would be Rs. 50,000 per annum. As this does not exceed the exemption limit, in each of the cases, no income tax would be payable by Ms. A or Ms. B or Ms. C. This is in contrast with the income tax of Rs. 19,000 with a rebate under section 88C of Rs. 5,000, i.e. Rs. 14,000 payable by her. It is assumed that the age of Ms. D at the time of the death was 56 years. Thus, a sum of Rs. 14,000 would be saved by way of income tax. Further, even if the incomes of Ms. A, Ms. B and Ms. C were upto Rs. 80,000 from the reinvestment of the fixed deposit receipts, none of them would be liable to income tax because of the rebate allowed to women of Rs. 5,000 under section 88C. Thus, through proper drafting of the will and making specific bequests to specific legatees, a lot of income tax can be saved in the hands of recipients of bequests through the will.

Legal Heirs vs Other Beneficiaries

The legal heirs for Hindus, whether male or female, are decided by provisions contained in the Hindu Succession Act. Section 8 of the Hindu Succession Act speaks about the general rules of succession in the case of a male Hindu dying intestate. Similarly, section 15 of the Hindu Succession Act speaks about the general rules of succession in the case of female Hindus dying intestate. Provisions under sections 8 and 15 of the Hindu Succession Act relating to the legal heirs are superseded where a person prepares a will and transfers his assets according to his desire. In case a person does not prepare a will and the assets are to be inherited by the legal heirs, then the system of inheritance by such legal heirs will be governed by the above mentioned provisions of the Hindu Succession Act.

It is clearly provided in section 8 of the Hindu Succession Act that the property of the male Hindu dying intestate shall be held according to the provisions of the Hindu

Succession Act in the following manner:

(a) Firstly, upon the heirs, being the relatives specified in Class I of the schedule;

(b) Secondly, if there is no heir of Class I, then upon the heirs, being the relatives specified in Class II of the schedule;

(c) Thirdly, if there is no heir of any of the two classes, then upon the agnates of the deceased; and

(d) Lastly, if there is no agnate, then upon the cognates of the deceased.

The Hindu Succession Act contains a schedule wherein the legal heirs are classified as Class I and Class II depending upon the relationship with the testator and his heirs.

The list of legal heirs in Class I and Class II follows.

Class I

I. Son, daughter, widow, mother.
II. Son of a predeceased son; daughter of a predeceased son.
III. Son of a predeceased daughter, daughter of a predeceased daughter.
IV. Widow of a predeceased son.
V. Son of a predeceased son of a predeceased son, daughter of a

predeceased son of a predeceased son; widow of a predeceased son of a predeceased son.

Class II

I. Father.

II. (1) Son's daughter's son, (2) Son's daughter's daughter, (3) Brother, (4) Sister.

III. (1) Daughter's son's son, (2) daughter's son's daughter, (3) daughter's daughter's son, (4) daughter's daughter's daughter.

IV. (1) Brother's son, (2) sister's son, (3) brother's daughter, (4) sister's daughter.

V. Father's father, father's mother.

VI. Father's widow, brother's widow

VII. Father's brother, father's sister

VIII. Mother's father, mother's mother.

IX. Mother's brother, mother's sister.

Explanation – In this schedule, references to a brother or sister do not include reference to a brother or sister by uterine blood.

In the absence of a will, the order of succession amongst the legal heirs starts as per the schedule mentioned above. Legal heirs that are listed in

Class I of the schedule qualify to become the legal heirs in the first place. Only when the legal heirs as mentioned in Class I are not present, do the legal heirs of Class II come into the picture. When Class II of the legal heirs are going to succeed the assets of a person dying intestate, then the succession process will start firstly with all the persons mentioned in entrylevel-I of Class II and thereafter entry No.II of Class II and so on. A male person whose legal heirs fall in the category in Class I of the schedule mentioned above will share the assets by giving one share to the widow. If there is more than one widow, then all the widows taken together will have one share. Likewise, the surviving sons and daughters and also the mother of the person dying intestate will each have a share. Likewise, all the legal heirs taken together in the lineage of each predeceased son or each predeceased daughter of the person, shall take one share between them. With regard to the property of a male person dying intestate, the sum shall be divided between the legal heirs in the second class of the schedule in any one entry, so that they share equally the assets of the person dying intestate.

It is clearly provided in the above mentioned section 8 of the Hindu Succession Act, that if the legal heirs in Class I and II are not present, then the assets of the deceased person dying intestate shall be given away to agnates.

Section 3 (1) of the Hindu Succession Act states that a person is stated to be an agnate of another person if the two are related by blood or adoption only through the male. For the purpose of this clause, relationship by blood, includes relationship by full blood, half blood and uterine blood. Agnates also include relatives by adoption.

Finally, the above mentioned section of the Hindu Succession Act states, that if there is no agnate, then the assets will devolve upon the cognates of the deceased. As per section 3(1) (c) of the Hindu Succession Act, a person is stated to be a cognate of another if the two are related by blood or adoption but not only through the male. For example, mother's brothers, son and brothers, daughters, would be treated as cognates.

Section 9 of the Hindu Succession Act states, that amongst the legal heirs specified in the schedule, those in Class I shall take simultaneously and to the exclusion of all other heirs: those in the first entry in Class-II shall be preferred to those in the second entry and so on.

The general rules for succession in the case of a Hindu female are contained in section 15 of the Hindu Succession Act. The property of a female Hindu dying intestate shall devolve in the following manner:

(a) Firstly, upon the sons and the daughters (including the children of any predeceased son or daughter), and also the husband;
(b) Secondly, upon the heirs of the husband;

(c) Thirdly, upon the mother and father;

(d) Fourthly, upon the heirs of the father; and

(e) Lastly, upon the heirs of the mother.

Thus, the assets belonging to the Hindu female who dies without executing a will, will be distributed as per the above mentioned section 15. Further it is provided in the section that:

(a) Any property inherited by a female Hindu from her father or mother shall devolve, in the absence of any son or daughter of the deceased (including the children of any predeceased son or daughter) not upon the other heirs referred to in sub-section (1) in the order specified therein, but upon the heirs of the father; and

(b) Any property inherited by a female Hindu from her husband or from her father-in-law shall devolve, in the absence of any son or daughter of the deceased (including the children of any predeceased son or daughter) not upon the other heirs referred to in sub-section (1) in the order specified therein, but upon the heirs of the husband.

With regard to succession a coparcenary property of Hindu Undivided Family, the provisions of succession in the event of a person dying intestate, are contained in section 6 of the Hindu Succession Act. It states that when a male Hindu dies having at the time of his death an interest in Mitakskra coparcenary property, his interest in the property shall devolve by survivorship upon surviving members of the coparcenary and not in accordance with the Hindu Succession Act. It is further mentioned in this section that provided if the deceased male had left surviving him a female relative specified in Class I of the schedule, or a male relative specified in this class who claims through such a female relative the interest of the deceased in the Mitakshra coparcenary, property shall devolve by testamentary or intestate succession, as the case may be, under provisions of Hindu Succession Act and not by survivorship. Further, it is mentioned in this section, that the interest of a Hindu Mitakshra coparcener will be deemed to be the share in the property that would have been allotted to him if the partition of the property had taken place.

Thus, if we undertake an in-depth study of the various provisions of inheritance as per the Hindu Succession Act, we come to the conclusion that the choice is with the individual whether to prepare his will or not to prepare his will. Even if a will is not prepared, the succession of the assets will take place but it will be exactly in tune with the provisions contained in the Hindu Succession Act. Whereas, if a will is prepared by a person, then all the provisions relating to inheritance as per the Hindu Succession Act will not be applicable. Rather the distribution of his assets will take place in the manner as he likes and to whosoever he likes, regardless of any law.

Thus the distribution of assets through a will is much easier and simpler and will give you a lot of satisfaction.

Conclusion

Having studied in the previous chapters, the importance of drafting a will and tax planning advantages attached to a will, it is recommended that all persons prepare a will. A supplementary will can be prepared where only certain paragraphs of a will are to be changed. To avoid confusion in the family and for smooth transfer of all the assets, it is strongly recommended that a will is prepared and preferably registered.

It must be noted that only self-acquired property can be WILLED AWAY. Ancestral property that a person enjoys cannot be WILLED AWAY. It has to abide by the Law of Succession.